W9-CMU-444

A sailor at Ford Island Naval Air Station in Hawaii watches as the USS *Shaw* explodes in the distance. He stands near planes destroyed by Japanese bombs.

Photographs © 2010: **Alamy Images/Douglas Peebles Photography:** 53; **AP Images:** back cover (Mary Naiden), 39 top (U.S. Marine Corps Forces, Pacific), 22 bottom, 55 top, 57; **Art Resource, NY/Bildarchiv Preussischer Kulturbesitz:** 8 foreground; **Australian War Memorial/Naval Historical Collection/Negative #305022:** 40 top; **Bridgeman Art Library International Ltd., London/New York/Private Collection/Peter Newark Military Pictures:** 26, 27; **Bureau of Medicine and Surgery Library and Archives:** 46 left (01-010), 47 top (01-019); **Corbis Images:** 18 top, 38, 43 top, 46 right (Bettmann), 7 top, 16 center (Museum of Flight), 48; **Everett Collection, Inc.:** 33 (©Touchstone Pictures), 24 bottom, 25 bottom (Keystone/Eyedea), 42; **Courtesy of the George DeLong Family:** 49 bottom; **Getty Images:** 50 bottom (Andrew Cooper SMPSP/Touchstone Pictures and Jerry Bruckheimer, Inc.), 47 bottom, 52 bottom (Henry Groskinsky/Time Life Pictures), 35 bottom, 56 (Hulton Archive), 14 bottom (Keystone), 54 bottom, 55 bottom (Dorothea Lange), 54 top (Thomas D. Mcavoy/Time Life Pictures), 50 top (Ralph Morse/Time Life Pictures), 9 top (Popperfoto), 44, 45 (Three Lions), 22 top (Time Life Pictures/National Archives); **Kobal Collection/Picture Desk:** 21 top (20th Century Fox), 23 (Andrew Cooper/Touchstone Pictures and Jerry Bruckheimer, Inc.); **Library of Congress, Prints and Photographs Division/Office of War Information Photograph Collection:** 52 top; **National Archives and Records Administration:** 16 bottom (80-G-345605), 16 top (80-G-427153), 2, 3 (Franklin D. Roosevelt Library/ARC 195303), cover (Franklin D. Roosevelt Library/ARC 196243); **Superstock, Inc.:** 5, 21 bottom, 39 bottom; **The Granger Collection, New York:** 8 background, 9 bottom, 10 (ullstein bild), 25 top, 31 top; **The Image Works/Roger-Viollet:** 14 top; **U.S. Naval Historical Center/Naval History & Heritage Command:** 40 bottom (80-G-19933), 51 (80-G-19941), 41 (80-G-19942), 34 (80-G-21743), 7 bottom, 28 right (80-G-408456), 17 top (80-G-413507), 15 (80-G-71198), 35 top (80-G-71586), 24 top (80-G-K-13512), 17 bottom (KN-2589), 32 bottom (NH 50472), 12, 13 (NH 50926), 28 left (NH 50930), 19 (NH 50931), 43 bottom (NH 62656), 32 top (NH 92310), 36 top (NH 95448), 36 bottom, 37 bottom (NH 97432), 18 bottom (NH 97446); **University of Hawaii at Manoa/Hawaii War Records Depository:** 1 (#126), 49 top (#615); **USS Arizona Memorial, NPS Collection:** 29, 31 bottom, 37 top.

Maps by David Lindroth, Inc.

Book design: Red Herring Design/NYC

Library of Congress Cataloging-in-Publication Data

Dougherty, Steve, 1948–
Pearl Harbor : the U.S. enters World War II / Steven Dougherty.
p. cm. — (24/7 goes to war)
Includes bibliographical references and index.
ISBN-13: 978-0-531-25525-4 (lib. bdg.) 978-0-531-25450-9 (pbk.)
ISBN-10: 0-531-25525-5 (lib. bdg.) 0-531-25450-X (pbk.)
1. Pearl Harbor (Hawaii), Attack on, 1941—Juvenile literature. 2. World War, 1939–1945—Causes—Juvenile literature. 3. Japan—foreign relations—United States—Juvenile literature. 4. United States—Foreign relations—Japan—Juvenile literature. I. Title.
D767.92.D67 2010
940.54'26693—dc22
2009020143

PEARL HARBOR

The U.S. Enters World War II

STEVE DOUGHERTY

Franklin Watts®
An Imprint of Scholastic Inc.

JAPANESE ATTACK FLEET

JAPANESE AIRCRAFT CARRIERS

PACIFIC OCEAN

JAPANESE AIRCRAFT
SQUADRONS

THE ATTACK ON PEARL HARBOR

On December 7, 1941, Japanese planes appeared over the Hawaiian island of Oahu and rained destruction on U.S. warships and air bases.

220 miles to Oahu

KEY

site of Japanese strike

0   5 mi.

0   5 km

FIRST WAVE

SECOND WAVE

NORTH

WEST   EAST

SOUTH

Haleiwa
Field

OAHU

Wheeler
Air Force Base

Kaneohe Naval
Air Station

Pearl
Harbor

Ford Island
Naval Air Station

Bellows
Field

Ewa
Field

Hickam
Field

Honolulu

Diamond
Head

President Franklin D. Roosevelt woke to the insistent ringing of his phone. It was before dawn on September 1, 1939, and the American ambassador in France was calling with urgent news. One and a half million German troops had invaded Poland.

Adolf Hitler, the dictator of Nazi Germany, had begun his campaign to conquer the democracies of Europe. "It has come at last," Roosevelt sighed. "God help us all."

Following the invasion, Great Britain and France organized an alliance—whose members were known as the Allies—to oppose the German threat. Although most Americans supported the Allies, they felt removed from the fighting. Many people—known as isolationists—wanted to stay out of the conflict. They were relieved when Roosevelt announced that the U.S. would "remain a neutral nation."

U.S. President Franklin D. Roosevelt

Out of Isolation

For nine months, Roosevelt's promise was easy to keep. Then in May and June 1940, Nazi tanks overran Belgium, the Netherlands, and France. Suddenly, Britain stood alone against the Nazi threat.

Roosevelt began to nudge his country out of isolation. In 1941, the U.S. started shipping guns, tanks, and planes across the Atlantic Ocean to Britain. Many ships were attacked by German U-boat subs. In October, a German torpedo sent a U.S. destroyer to the ocean floor. "Only the thinnest of lines separates the United States from war," Roosevelt declared.

A German U-boat in 1941

9

But for the U.S., the war would begin in the Pacific Ocean, not the Atlantic.

For many years, the U.S. and powerful countries in Europe had controlled the Pacific region south of Japan. Now Japan, under the leadership of Prime Minister Hideki Tojo, was determined to become the dominant power in Asia.

However, Japan was a small nation and didn't have the resources to carry out its plans. It needed iron for weapons, rubber for tires, and coal and oil for fuel. In July 1937, Japan had launched a brutal invasion of China to capture its coal and iron reserves.

Three years later, Japan took two more threatening steps. It sent troops into French Indochina (present-day Vietnam and Cambodia). It also joined an alliance—called the Axis—with Germany and Italy.

Japanese leaders then made plans to move into British Malaya, the Dutch East Indies, and the U.S.-dominated Philippines. These areas would provide Japan with much of the rubber and oil it needed.

Japanese troops cheer after capturing a Chinese train station in 1937.

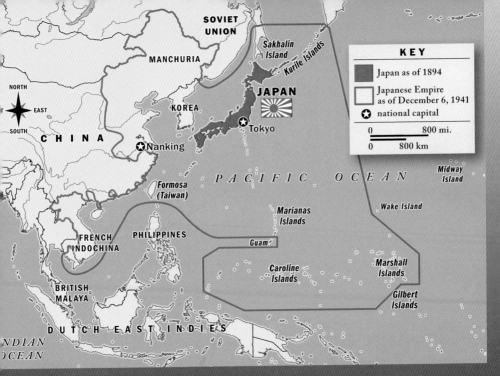

KEY

Japan as of 1894

Japanese Empire as of December 6, 1941

⭘ national capital

0   800 mi.

0   800 km

JAPANESE EXPANSION BEFORE PEARL HARBOR

By late 1941, Japan's empire stretched into China, Southeast Asia, and the Pacific.

As the Japanese grew bolder, the U.S. began to push back. Roosevelt banned the sale of steel, scrap iron, and oil to Japan. He also demanded the withdrawal of Japanese troops from China. And Roosevelt made a move that Japan found especially threatening. He ordered the U.S. Pacific Fleet to relocate from San Diego, California, to Pearl Harbor, Hawaii. That put the fleet 2,500 miles closer to Japan.

Japan's leaders began to devise a plan to prevent the mighty U.S. Navy from interfering with their grand scheme. Japanese warplanes would launch a surprise attack on the U.S. fleet at Pearl Harbor.

Late in November, American pilots sighted half the Japanese fleet steaming south toward the Philippines and Malaya. But the rest of Japan's warships were nowhere to be seen.

In fact, hidden beneath thick clouds, the missing aircraft carriers were headed toward Hawaii. Their radios were turned off to prevent the U.S. Navy from detecting their presence.

Onboard the carriers was a strike force of 353 warplanes.

11

Shortly after the Japanese attack on Pearl Harbor, U.S. Marines sit in shock near their barracks. In the background, smoke rises from burning ships.

RUCK AT DAWN

It was a quiet Sunday morning in Pearl Harbor. Then suddenly the sky was filled with Japanese warplanes.

Commander Mitsuo Fuchida awoke before dawn and began to prepare for battle. It was December 7, 1941. In just a few hours, he would lead 353 planes from the Japanese Imperial Navy in a surprise attack on the U.S. Pacific Fleet at Pearl Harbor, a huge naval base on the Hawaiian island of Oahu.

Japanese pilots receive instructions before taking off for Pearl Harbor.

Fuchida was on the aircraft carrier *Akagi*. It was one of six Japanese carriers that had crossed the Pacific Ocean. Now the fleet was within striking distance of Pearl Harbor, just 220 miles away.

Fuchida dressed with care. First, he put on a red shirt. That way, if he were hit, his men wouldn't be able to tell that he was bleeding. Next, he pulled on his flight suit and tied a scarf around his head. On the scarf was a large red dot—the Rising Sun symbol of Japan—and the word *Hisso!* It meant "Certain Victory!"

An hour later, as rough seas battered the carriers, 183 planes began to take off. They were the first wave of the strike force—a second wave of 170 planes would soon follow.

As the planes rose into the sky, sailors on the decks cheered their comrades on to victory. By 6:20 A.M., all the planes were in the air, and Fuchida ordered his pilots to begin the 90-minute flight to Oahu.

Commander Mitsuo Fuchida led the raid on the U.S. Pacific Fleet.

Japanese planes prepare to take off from an aircraft carrier to attack Pearl Harbor. The strike force was armed with machine guns, bombs, and torpedoes.

Their mission was part of Japan's strategy to expand its empire throughout the Pacific. To make sure the U.S. wouldn't be able to interfere, Prime Minister Hideki Tojo ordered the destruction of U.S. warships and bombers at Pearl Harbor.

As the planes neared Oahu, Fuchida was feeling confident. Visibility was good; his pilots would have a clear view of their targets. And Fuchida hadn't seen any U.S. spotter planes, which meant that his strike force hadn't been discovered.

"A more favorable situation [for the attack] could not have been imagined," Fuchida later recalled.

Pearl Harbor Sleeps

As the warplanes flew toward Oahu, most people at Pearl Harbor were still asleep.

It was a beautiful Sunday morning. Many servicemen and women planned to spend the day off at the beach.

U.S. leaders knew that war with Japan might come at any time. But few believed that Pearl Harbor would be attacked. After all, it was 4,000 miles from Japan, and it would be difficult for a strike force to cross the Pacific undetected. It seemed more

THE JAPANESE STRIKE FORCE

Japanese pilots flew these aircraft during the attack on Pearl Harbor.

NAKAJIMA B5N BOMBER (Allied code name: "Kate"):
Some of these bombers were armed with torpedoes specially designed for Pearl Harbor's shallow waters. Others carried bombs that were dropped from high altitudes.

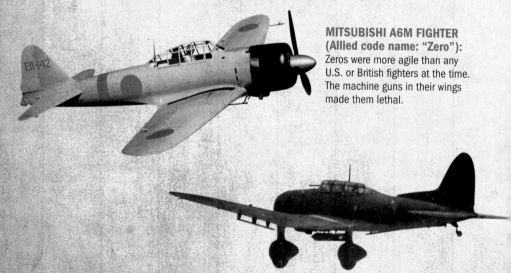

MITSUBISHI A6M FIGHTER (Allied code name: "Zero"):
Zeros were more agile than any U.S. or British fighters at the time. The machine guns in their wings made them lethal.

AICHI D3A DIVE BOMBER (Allied code name: "Val")
Val bombers streaked down out of the sky and came in low to hit their targets. The plane carried a big bomb under its fuselage and a smaller bomb under each wing. Vals were more accurate than high-altitude bombers, but they were also more vulnerable.

This map of Pearl Harbor was found in a captured Japanese sub.

This Japanese midget submarine sank while attacking Pearl Harbor. Only two sailors fit inside the tiny vessel.

likely that Japan would hit the British and Dutch colonies in Southeast Asia, or the U.S.-dominated Philippines.

Even if a Japanese fleet *did* get close to Pearl Harbor, U.S. commanders were sure that warning systems would alert them in time to mobilize their defenses.

They were partly right. Lookouts did see the Japanese coming. And they did alert their commanders.

But the warnings were ignored.

The first sign of trouble came at 6:30 A.M., when a sailor on the destroyer USS *Ward* spotted a midget submarine near the harbor entrance. He quickly sounded the alarm: "Enemy sub!"

The men on the *Ward* didn't know it, but the sub was one of five midget subs trying to sneak into the harbor. They had been ordered to shoot torpedoes at the U.S. ships in the harbor once the aerial assault began.

The *Ward* opened fire and struck the midget sub. When the sub dove to get away, the *Ward* blew it up with depth charges—bombs that detonate underwater.

The *Ward*'s captain immediately reported the incident. But the commander who received the message waited too long to pass it on.

Private Joseph Lockard detected the Japanese strike force on his radar screen. But his warning was ignored.

Another warning came around 7:00 A.M. On the northern tip of Oahu, Private Joseph Lockard was manning his radar station. Suddenly, he saw some blips on his screen, indicating a large number of planes within 100 miles. He immediately called his commander. "It's the largest [group of planes] I have ever seen," Lockard exclaimed.

But Lockard's commander wasn't worried. He thought the blips were a squadron of U.S. bombers due in from California. "Don't worry about it," he told Lockard. "It's nothing." The officer would regret those words.

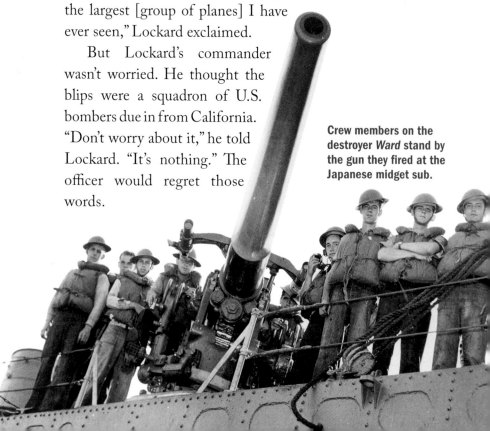
Crew members on the destroyer *Ward* stand by the gun they fired at the Japanese midget sub.

This photo of Battleship Row was taken from a Japanese plane during the first minutes of the attack. The rings in the water were caused by a torpedo strike.

"Tora! Tora! Tora!"

Commander Mitsuo Fuchida couldn't believe his eyes.

A few miles ahead, the U.S. Pacific Fleet lay peacefully at anchor. Fuchida could see seven battleships lined up on "Battleship Row." They looked "like toys on a child's floor," one of his pilots said.

At 7:49 A.M., Fuchida radioed the order to attack: "*To! To! To!*" The strike force split up into groups, with some planes heading toward the airfields scattered across the island and others diving toward the harbor, their engines screaming.

Fuchida scanned the sky. No American planes were rising up to defend the ships. There was no anti-aircraft fire. He quickly radioed a message to his commanders: "*Tora! Tora! Tora!*"

The code phrase meant that the attack had caught the Americans completely by surprise.

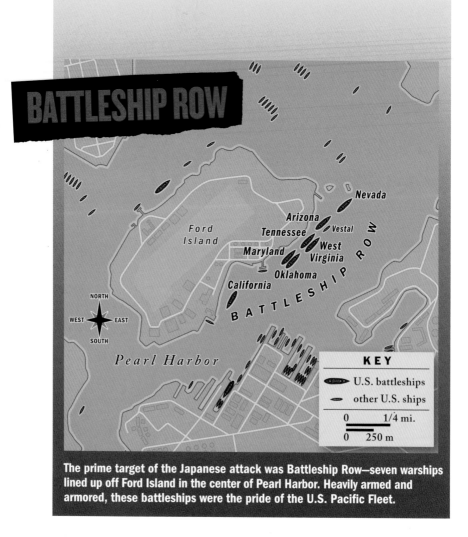

BATTLESHIP ROW

Nevada

Arizona
Tennessee · Vestal
West
Maryland Virginia
Oklahoma
California

Ford
Island

NORTH
WEST — EAST
SOUTH

Pearl Harbor

B A T T L E S H I P   R O W

KEY

U.S. battleships

other U.S. ships

| 0 | 1/4 mi. |
| 0 | 250 m |

The prime target of the Japanese attack was Battleship Row—seven warships lined up off Ford Island in the center of Pearl Harbor. Heavily armed and armored, these battleships were the pride of the U.S. Pacific Fleet.

"This Is No Drill!"

It was a peaceful and beautiful morning in Pearl Harbor.

Waves were lapping gently against the docks, and the sound of a band playing the "Star-Spangled Banner" drifted across the water.

Suddenly, the calm was shattered by the shriek of diving airplanes. Bombers appeared above the harbor, flying low over Battleship Row. Fighters and dive bombers swooped down on nearby airfields, their crews intent on destroying the planes before American pilots could take off and defend the fleet.

At first, civilians in pajamas and sleepy sailors finishing their pancakes thought they were witnessing an American air show.

In this shot from the 1970 movie *Tora! Tora! Tora!*, Japanese torpedo bombers descend on the U.S. Pacific Fleet at Pearl Harbor.

"This is the best drill the Army Air Force has ever put on," marveled one sailor.

"What a stupid, careless pilot!" a U.S. admiral thought when a plane dropped a bomb near the battleships. Then he saw the plane's Rising Sun insignia. "Japanese!" he shouted. "Man your stations!"

A few seconds later, an announcement came over the loudspeakers: "Air raid, Pearl Harbor! This is no drill!" There was no longer any doubt—Pearl Harbor was under attack.

Nearby, at Wheeler Field, Japanese pilots were "bombing

These barracks on Ford Island, Pearl Harbor, were hit by Japanese bombs.

As bombs fall on Kaneohe Bay Naval Air Station, a sailor runs for cover.

and strafing . . . the planes, the officers' quarters, even the golf course!" one witness said. Hundreds of airmen were killed when bombs fell on their barracks.

Wrecked U.S. planes lie on a runway at Hickam Field.

At Hickam Field, dozens of B-17 bombers were destroyed in a single devastating attack. "Dive bombers were tearing the place to pieces," a witness reported.

Fighter planes flew low over the airfields, their machine guns blazing. They fired at men running for safety, at parked planes, at hangars and warehouses and dining halls.

Nearly every plane on the island was damaged or destroyed. Only a few pilots were able to take off and fight the enemy.

"It was a pitiful, unholy mess," said one air-base commander.

A Direct Hit

Japanese planes screamed over Battleship Row, dropping bombs and torpedoes.

On the USS *Oklahoma*, sailors watched helplessly as a bomber swooped down and released a torpedo. The propeller-driven bomb hit the water and shot forward as if fired from a gun.

The torpedo struck the *Oklahoma* dead center and exploded. The huge battleship rocked violently. "I felt a heavy shock and heard a loud explosion," the ship's executive officer said later.

"Then slowly, sickeningly, the *Oklahoma* began to roll over on her side," a witness said. Some crewmen were able to climb the tilting deck and jump into the harbor. Many were horribly burned by fires blazing on the oil-covered water.

"Men were screaming and trying to get aboard our ship," said one sailor. "The harbor was aflame. The smoke and fire was all around us."

Within minutes, the *Oklahoma* had turned all the way over, and only its hull could be seen.

More than 400 sailors were trapped inside.

In this scene from the movie *Pearl Harbor*, a Japanese fighter attacks U.S. warships.

The *Arizona* Explodes

Deafening explosions shook the harbor as other ships were hit. The sound of gunfire and screams filled the air.

Ships seemed to "explode in a chain reaction," said a boy who witnessed the attacks on Battleship Row.

The pride of the U.S. Pacific Fleet, the USS *Arizona*, suffered a devastating hit when an armor-piercing bomb ripped through the ship's upper decks and exploded in its ammunition hold.

The *Arizona* erupts in a fireball after being hit by a Japanese bomb.

"That big *Arizona* blew up like a million Fourth of Julys," said one witness. Sailors were blown into the air. The "legs, arms, and heads of men" rained down on the decks of a ship tied up next to the *Arizona*.

Hundreds of crewmen on the *Arizona* were killed instantly. Hundreds more died in the fires that burned out of control. Others were blown off the ship and drowned. Some who swam to shore were "burned like lamb chops," a survivor reported. "They were moaning, walking around in a daze."

"Great Ships Were Dying"

Suddenly, less than an hour after the attack began, Fuchida's planes turned and flew off.

Rescuers and medical workers rushed to free trapped sailors and care for the wounded.

But the lull was brief.

Just before 9:00 A.M., a second wave of planes arrived, and the bombing resumed. This time, the attackers met more resistance. American pilots and ground gunners shot down 29 Japanese planes.

By 9:45 A.M., less than two hours after the first bombs fell, the attack was over. The casualties were staggering: 2,433 dead; 1,178 wounded.

The *Arizona* sank in less than nine minutes, and 1,177 of the sailors onboard were killed.

Five great battleships had been sunk or badly damaged. Many other warships had been crippled. And 347 planes had been damaged or destroyed. Japan had succeeded in putting much of the U.S. Pacific Fleet out of action.

Mrs. John Earle had watched the attack from a hillside overlooking Pearl Harbor. When it was all over, she stood in shock, looking down at the burning and sinking ships.

"It was awful," she said later. "Great ships were dying before my eyes. . . [and] men were dying too."

After the attack, anti-aircraft gunners keep watch in case of another raid.

2

FIGHT

ING BACK

Japanese fighters swooped down out of the sky, their guns blazing. Disregarding their own safety, hundreds of U.S. soldiers, sailors, and airmen fought back.

U.S. troops defend an airfield near Pearl Harbor on December 7, 1941.

Mess Attendant Doris "Dorie" Miller was leaving the ship's laundry when an explosion knocked him off his feet. The tremendous blast sent shock waves through the USS *West Virginia*.

Miller heard sailors shouting that the battleship was under attack. Enemy planes were bombing the fleet! It was hard to believe. Just moments before, the 22-year-old had been looking forward to finishing his shift and enjoying the rest of the day.

As a mess attendant, Miller worked in the ship's kitchen and dining rooms. When the bomb hit, he'd just dropped off table linens at the laundry.

Now, as he made his way along the passageway, he heard wounded men screaming. And he saw the dead bodies of shipmates who had been trading jokes just moments ago.

The passageway was filling with thick black smoke. Miller inched along, searching for a way to the main deck.

When he got there, he couldn't believe his eyes.

The gigantic ship was leaning to one side.

Its towering masts were bent and broken.

The ship's huge cannons looked like toy

This photo was taken from a Japanese plane. It shows the moment the *West Virginia* was hit by a torpedo. At right, Dorie Miller in 1942.

models that had been stomped on and crushed. And everywhere, fires burned out of control.

Looking up, Miller saw fighter planes buzzing Battleship Row, where the *West Virginia* and six other battleships were moored. Low-flying bombers released torpedoes that shot through the water. Several hit the *West Virginia*, blowing huge holes in its side.

As the *West Virginia* burns, a small boat comes to the rescue of sailors who jumped overboard.

Sailors with their clothes on fire desperately tried to put out the flames. Wounded men moaned in agony. There were dead bodies everywhere, some with their arms and legs blown off. The ship's deck was slick with blood.

Worse was yet to come. For the next two hours, the U.S. fleet was pounded by bombs and strafed by machine guns. But Miller and countless other servicemen didn't give up.

They fought back.

Attack on Wheeler Field

Army pilots George S. Welch and Kenneth M. Taylor had been out all night.

On Saturday evening, they had put on tuxedos and gone to a formal dance at the Officers' Club at Wheeler Field. Then they'd joined an all-night poker game.

Now it was early Sunday morning. The game was over, and Welch and Taylor were debating whether to go to bed or head out for a swim.

Suddenly, they heard an explosion. At first they thought it was bombing practice. But once the men stepped outside, they realized that Wheeler Field was under attack.

THE FLEET AT
PEARL HARBOR

Since early 1940, Pearl Harbor had been home to the massive U.S. Pacific Fleet. On December 7, 1941, about 18,000 sailors, soldiers, airmen, doctors, nurses, and other military personnel were based there. There were about 130 ships in the harbor and hundreds of planes at nearby airfields. Here's a look at some of them.

SHIPS

8	battleships	These large and powerful vessels had thick armor, and their giant cannons could pound the enemy from miles away.
8	cruisers	Cruisers were smaller than battleships. Some guarded aircraft carriers; others were used to attack enemy ships.
30	destroyers	Fast and compact, destroyers escorted larger warships and protected them from submarines, torpedo boats, and other attackers.
14	minesweepers	These small warships were used to find and destroy mines placed in the water by enemy minelayers.
1	hospital ship	This floating hospital provided medical care for sick or injured sailors and soldiers.

PLANES

113	bombers	Among them were 12 B-17D Flying Fortresses. They got their name because they were so well armored. These bombers could fly 3,400 miles without refueling and carry a 4,800-pound bomb load.
200	fighter planes	These included 23 F4F-3 Wildcats, the most common carrier-based fighter at the time. Because of their heavy armor, they could survive more damage than lighter planes like the Japanese Zero.
105	amphibious planes	Fifty-four of these were PBY-5 Catalina "flying boats." Their many functions included attacking submarines and rescuing downed pilots from the sea.

Japanese Zero fighters screamed overhead, their machine guns blazing. Kate dive bombers swooped in, dropping bombs on the neat rows of American planes.

Wheeler was one of five air bases dedicated to protecting the U.S. fleet at Pearl Harbor. By disabling the planes at these airfields, the Japanese were making it impossible for U.S. pilots to fight back.

But Taylor and Welch thought they had a shot at getting in the air. Their P-40 Warhawk fighter planes were at least ten miles away, at Haleiwa Field, an airstrip so small it didn't appear on most maps.

A Japanese fighter attacks a U.S. airfield.

Taylor ran through a hail of machine-gun bullets to get to his car, while Welch rushed to call Haleiwa. A crewman there told him that the airfield wasn't under attack—at least, not yet.

Taylor pulled up in his car and Welch jumped in. They sped away, weaving around burning airplanes. When they reached Haleiwa, they wheeled to a stop and ran to their planes.

Still dressed in their tuxedos, the two pilots took off.

Smoke pours from an airplane hangar at Kaneohe Bay Naval Air Station.

USS *Vestal* Bombed

Cassin Young was belowdecks when two bombs struck his ship, the *Vestal*.

Cassin Young, commanding officer of the *Vestal*

The *Vestal* was a small repair ship moored alongside the *Arizona* in Battleship Row. Commanding Officer Young immediately raced for the bridge—the raised command center of the ship. There, he grabbed an anti-aircraft gun and started shooting at the Japanese fighter planes overhead.

A moment later, an armor-piercing bomb plunged through the upper decks of the battleship *Arizona*. The bomb exploded in the *Arizona*'s ammunition hold. The shock wave from the explosion was so powerful that it blew Young and others from the *Vestal* overboard.

As the bewildered sailors treaded water, they "could see the men on [the] *Arizona* . . . burning alive," one *Vestal* officer remembered. "They were a ghostly crew as they walked out of those flames. And then they just dropped dead."

Within minutes, fires from the *Arizona* leaped over to the *Vestal*. The remaining crew prepared to abandon ship.

Meanwhile, Young had managed to swim back to his ship and climb aboard. Dripping wet and covered in oil, he ordered his sailors to stay put. The *Vestal* could still be saved, he told them.

Moments later, a torpedo bomber turned toward the *Vestal*.

An aerial shot of Battleship Row just after the attack began. The *Vestal* (circled) is alongside the *Arizona*.

This shot from the 2001 movie *Pearl Harbor* shows Japanese fighters attacking U.S. sailors.

Young and one of his officers watched as a torpedo dropped from the plane, hit the water, and streaked forward—straight at them. The two men glanced at each other. "Good-bye," Young said to the officer.

"Good-bye, Captain," the officer replied.

Defending the *West Virginia*

Two bombs and five torpedoes had slammed into the *West Virginia*. Seawater was pouring in through gaping holes in the hull.

On the main deck, fires were raging. But Mess Attendant Dorie Miller ignored the danger and rushed to move wounded sailors to safer sections of the ship.

Then Miller heard a call for help. It came from a gunner who was manning one of two big Browning .50-caliber machine guns. The sailor operating the second gun had been killed, and somebody had to take his place.

An officer standing nearby grabbed the second gun and ordered Miller to feed him ammunition.

A moment later, a bullet struck and killed the first gunner.

Miller froze. His instincts told him to take over. But he had no training with anti-aircraft guns—or any other heavy weapons. As an African American sailor, he was permitted to assist gunners; he wasn't allowed to fire the guns himself.

In 1941, African Americans in the U.S. Navy were restricted to low-level jobs, such as working in the ship's laundry and kitchen, or assisting officers. They weren't trained for combat and couldn't rise through the ranks to become officers. "If you were black," recalled one mess attendant, "you could only be a servant."

Still, Miller had watched closely at gunnery school as white sailors learned to fire Browning .50-caliber guns. And he was a great shot with a hunting rifle.

As diving Zeros sprayed the deck with bullets, Miller climbed into the gunner's seat. He grabbed hold of the gun, took aim, and opened fire.

In 1942, the U.S. Navy began to allow African Americans to take on combat roles. These sailors were among the first to serve on a gun crew.

A sailor takes his turn firing a 20-mm machine gun during a training session onboard the aircraft carrier USS *Copahee* in 1942.

Dogfight!

Welch and Taylor jumped into their P-40 Warhawk fighters.

The ground crew had gotten the planes gassed up, armed, and ready for battle in record time. The two young pilots took off. Climbing high over Oahu, they searched the skies for enemy fighters. Soon, they spotted squadrons of Japanese planes far below.

Welch and Taylor were vastly outnumbered, but they didn't hesitate. With machine guns blazing, the pilots dove straight at the enemy and shot down two dive bombers. Then they spotted another group of enemy planes and took off after them.

Two P-40 Warhawk fighter planes flying in formation

In one duel with a Japanese fighter, Taylor was wounded, and his P-40 was badly shot up. Still, the 21-year-old pilot managed to shoot down his adversary.

At one point, Taylor took on a group of planes in a series of dizzying dogfights over the beach at Waialua. "I got [caught] in a string of six or eight planes," he recalled later. "I was on one plane's tail . . . and there was one following, firing at me."

Taylor tried to lose the plane behind him, but he couldn't get rid of it. He was sure he was a goner.

Then his friend Welch zoomed in and blasted the Japanese plane out of the sky.

Shootout on the Airfields

John Finn stood on a runway at the Kaneohe air base, blasting away with a machine gun.

A Zero was diving right at him, but Chief Petty Officer Finn wasn't thinking about his own safety.

"Our hangars were burning, our planes were exploding where they sat, and men were dying," Finn recalled years later. "I was so mad, I didn't have time to be afraid."

At Kaneohe and other U.S. airfields on Oahu, soldiers were determined to fight back. But the bases' powerful anti-aircraft weapons had been locked up weeks before—to prevent sabotage by spies. Servicemen had to make do with

John Finn with the Medal of Honor he received for his heroism on December 7

Armed only with rifles, U.S. Marines try to defend Ewa Airfield.

rifles and even handguns, or with machine guns torn out of destroyed planes.

At Wheeler Field, Lieutenant Stephen Saltzman grabbed a rifle and aimed it at a low-flying Zero. The pilot fired back with his four machine guns. But Saltzman "had a perfect shot at the pilot," he said later. He pulled the trigger and a moment later, the Zero crashed nearby.

Sailors struggle to save a plane that was damaged during the Japanese attack on the Kaneohe airfield.

THE P-40 WARHAWK

It was the economy car of fighter planes. The P-40 Warhawk wasn't glamorous, but it got the job done. About half the planes at Pearl Harbor were P-40s. Allied countries such as Britain, Australia, China, and the USSR also flew P-40s.

Here's a look at why some pilots loved these fighters—and others hated them.

P-40 STATS

SEATS: 1
ENGINES: 1 (1,000 to 1,200 horsepower)
TOP SPEED: 340 mph
TOP ALTITUDE: 30,000 feet
WEIGHT: 8,058 pounds

STRENGTHS

SPEED: The P-40 could outrun the Japanese Zero, allowing U.S. pilots to escape dogfights when they were in trouble.

FIREPOWER: The aircraft was armed with two powerful .50-caliber machine guns and four .30-caliber machine guns.

AIR SUPPORT: The P-40 had thick armor and flew best at low altitudes, so it was often used to provide cover fire for troops on the ground.

COST: The plane was cheap to build. Almost 14,000 P-40s were built between 1939 and 1944.

GOOD TRACK RECORD: In early 1941, the Flying Tigers—a group of Americans piloting P-40s—volunteered to fight the Japanese in China. Although the Tigers were outnumbered, they shot down about 400 enemy aircraft while losing just 12 P-40s in combat.

WEAKNESSES

CLUMSY: The P-40 was heavy for a fighter plane, which meant it was clumsy at low speeds. It couldn't turn or climb nearly as quickly as the lightweight Zero.

SHORT RANGE: The P-40 couldn't fly very far without refueling. It was eventually replaced by the P-38, which allowed the U.S. to strike targets deep inside enemy territory.

The Allies used P-40s in the Pacific, North Africa, and Eastern Europe.

Lt. Fusata Iida died when his plane was shot down by a U.S. Navy airman.

Back at Kaneohe, a Navy airman named Sands took on Lieutenant Fusata Iida, the daring commander of a Japanese fighter group.

Armed only with a Browning Automatic Rifle (BAR), Sands stood out in the open as Iida flew straight for him, his machine guns blazing.

Sands emptied his gun firing at Iida's plane. Then, after the Zero passed overhead, Sands shouted to a colleague, "Hand me another BAR! Hurry up!"

Once again, Sands stood his ground as Iida dove straight toward him. As bullets slammed into the wall behind him, Sands took careful aim and fired.

Gasoline poured from the tail of Iida's plane. The Japanese pilot turned to make a final attack, but the duel was over. A moment later, his bullet-riddled plane crashed to the ground.

This Zero fighter was one of 29 Japanese aircraft shot down on December 7. Almost 350 U.S. planes were destroyed or damaged during the attack.

Saving the *Vestal*

Commanding Officer Young braced for the explosion as a torpedo streaked toward his ship.

A torpedo from a Japanese midget submarine

Then he and one of his officers watched in amazement as the torpedo shot beneath the *Vestal* and struck the battleship *Arizona*. The blast was so powerful that it snuffed out most of the fires on the *Vestal*. But Young knew that to save his ship, he'd have to move it far from the burning *Arizona*.

With the bomb-damaged *Vestal* taking on more water every minute, Young managed to maneuver it across the harbor. Then, to keep it from sinking, he ran it aground.

"Despite severe enemy bombing . . . and his shocking experience of having been blown overboard," a military official wrote later, "Commander Young, with extreme coolness and calmness, [was able to] save his ship."

The *Vestal* after the attack. Commanding Officer Cassin Young saved the ship from sinking by running it aground.

The *Arizona* burns after being hit by torpedoes and bombs. When a bomb exploded in the battleship's ammunition hold, the powerful shock wave blew sailors off the decks of the nearby *Vestal*.

Cuba Gooding Jr. as Dorie Miller in a scene from the movie *Pearl Harbor*

"Extraordinary Courage"

Dorie Miller kept firing at the enemy planes attacking his ship.

Many sailors onboard the *West Virginia* prepared to abandon ship. But Miller remained at his anti-aircraft gun, exposed to enemy bullets and the searing heat of fires burning around him.

A Japanese plane suddenly dove straight at him. It was coming in so low that Miller could see the pilot's face. The pilot fired his guns, and bullets slammed into the ship's armor.

Miller took aim. The big .50-caliber gun bucked and kicked as he fired, but Miller held it steady.

Unleashing a final volley at Miller, the pilot pulled up and tried to soar away. But the plane had been hit. With smoke spewing from its tail, the aircraft spiraled into the harbor.

Firefighters work to contain a blaze after the Japanese attack on Pearl Harbor.

Lieutenant Ruth Erickson loved being a nurse in the U.S. Naval Hospital at Pearl Harbor. Most sailors were young and healthy, so the work was easy. She and her friends would spend their days off at the beach. They'd often go dancing at night.

It was a fun time—"another segment in my life's adventure," she said later.

On the morning of December 7, Erickson was eating breakfast with friends. "Suddenly we heard planes roaring overhead," she recalled. She dashed to the window and saw a low-flying plane swoop by. A Rising Sun insignia was painted on its wing.

Erickson knew what that meant—the plane was Japanese. "This is the real thing!" the head nurse yelled.

Her heart racing, Erickson ran across the street to the hospital. "Shrapnel was falling all over the place," she said. "Why I did not get hit, I do not know."

All over Pearl Harbor, rescue workers and medical personnel

An emergency aid station on December 7, 1941

like Erickson were braving bullets and flames to help their comrades. Soldiers and sailors searched for survivors and moved them to safety. Civilians pulled badly burned men out of the harbor and brought them to the hospitals. And medical teams worked frantically to save lives.

Lt. Ruth Erickson in 1941

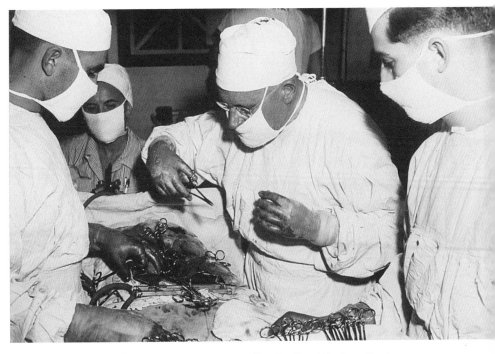

A U.S. Navy doctor performs emergency surgery after the Pearl Harbor attacks.

Erickson's first patient was bleeding from a terrible stomach wound. Doctors tried to help him, but he "died within the hour," she recalled. Soon, wounded soldiers and sailors were pouring into the hospital. At one point, a Japanese plane crashed right outside, but Erickson kept working.

Many of Erickson's patients were burn victims. She treated their burns and gave them morphine for the pain. "I can still smell [the burned flesh]," she said many years later, "and I think I always will."

For weeks after the

This blood-soaked uniform was worn by a pharmacist at Pearl Harbor.

attacks, Erickson and her colleagues continued to work around the clock. The medical workers at Pearl Harbor "rose to the challenge of that terrible emergency and performed miracles," Erickson recalled. "The attack brought the very best out of them."

A Glimmer of Hope

Julio DeCastro stood on the hull of the overturned USS *Oklahoma*, listening for knocking sounds.

During the attacks that morning, the battleship had been hit by torpedoes, causing it to capsize. Hundreds of sailors had been trapped inside. Now they were desperately trying to signal rescuers by banging on the walls of the ship.

DeCastro was a foreman at the Pearl Harbor Navy Yard, where the Pacific fleet's ships were repaired. As soon as the bombing was over, he had pulled together a rescue team of 21 shipyard workers and rushed to the *Oklahoma*.

Rescue workers on the hull of the capsized *Oklahoma* try to reach sailors trapped inside.

Julio DeCastro (seated) with family. He helped rescue sailors on the *Oklahoma*.

Standing on the capsized ship, DeCastro's team prepared to cut through the hull with air-powered drills and chisels. It would have been faster to use welding torches. But earlier, rescue workers had used a welding torch—with tragic results.

The rescuers had been cutting into a compartment where two sailors were trapped. As a welder burned through the metal wall, the torch's flame quickly used up all the oxygen in the small space. The sailors had suffocated.

DeCastro's crew wouldn't make the same mistake. Armed with air-powered tools, they began cutting through the thick steel hull.

Trapped inside the ship, 19-year-old George DeLong heard the drilling. He had been pounding on the walls with a wrench for hours. So far, the only response had been the knocking of other trapped sailors. Now, suddenly, there was a glimmer of hope.

Trapped!

That day, DeLong had been planning to go to the beach.

But as he climbed out of his bunk, a tremendous explosion had knocked him to the floor of the compartment that he shared with seven other sailors. More blasts followed, and the ship began to shake and shudder.

George DeLong, 19, was among the hundreds of sailors trapped inside the *Oklahoma*.

Sleeping quarters inside a U.S. Navy ship during World War II

"We didn't know what the explosions were," DeLong recalled later.

Just then, the door to their compartment slammed shut. In an emergency, sailors were supposed to shut all the doorways on the ship. That way, if the ship's hull had been pierced, leaks would be contained to the damaged area. A panicked sailor had locked the door to DeLong's compartment without checking inside. Now the eight sailors were trapped.

Suddenly, the ship began to roll over. DeLong held tight to his bunk as tools and machinery crashed around him. Within a few minutes, the ship was upside down.

Then the lights went out, and water began pouring in around DeLong's feet.

This scene from the movie *Pearl Harbor* shows the *Oklahoma* capsizing.

An Underwater Prison

Seawater flooded into the compartment through the air vent.

DeLong and the other trapped sailors stuffed a mattress into the opening, but as the hours passed, the water kept rising.

The air became hot and stale. The men were using up the available oxygen, and they were becoming weak. DeLong could barely lift the wrench he'd been using to signal for help.

Then suddenly, he heard drilling. The sailors banged on the walls, trying to guide the rescuers toward them.

Soon, the drilling was right over the sailors' heads. Light filled the room as the rescuers aimed a flashlight through a hole they'd cut into the compartment. DeLong felt a rush of relief.

The rescue team quickly lifted DeLong and his shipmates to safety. The sailors stood on the *Oklahoma*'s hull, taking big gulps of fresh air—and staring in shock at the wreckage of Pearl Harbor.

During the next few days, DeCastro's team and other rescuers managed to save 24 more men who'd been trapped in the *Oklahoma*. The bodies of 429 other sailors were later recovered from the ship.

Rescue workers search for sailors inside the *Oklahoma*.

DeLong had been trapped for 32 hours, but he had kept his cool in a terrifying situation. "I never felt that I was a hero," he said later. "I was a survivor. The fellows who rescued us were the heroes."

Diving In

John Garcia's grandmother shook him awake. *Pearl Harbor is under attack,* **she kept repeating.**

But even though Garcia could hear loud explosions nearby, he didn't believe her. It had to be U.S. troops conducting drills, the 16-year-old insisted.

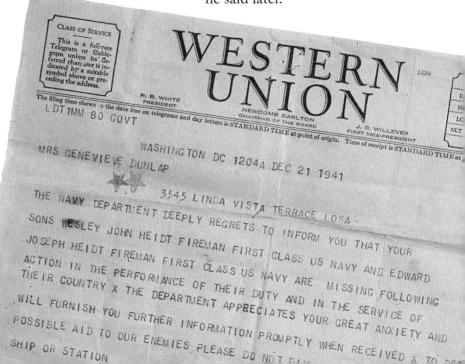

Then he saw black smoke rising above the harbor.

Garcia jumped on his motorbike and raced to the harbor. The surface of the water was covered with sailors. Some had jumped off burning ships. Others had been blown overboard by the blasts of exploding bombs.

Garcia immediately dove into the water to help. All day long and into the night he pulled men from the water. "I don't know how many . . . were alive and how many dead," he said later.

Firefighters work to save the *West Virginia*.

CLASS OF SERVICE

This is a full-rate Telegram or Cable-gram unless its de-ferred character is in-dicated by a suitable symbol above or pre-ceding the address.

WESTERN UNION

R. B. WHITE
PRESIDENT

NEWCOMB CARLTON
CHAIRMAN OF THE BOARD

J. C. WILLEVER
FIRST VICE-PRESIDENT

1220

The filing time shown in the date line on telegrams and day letters is STANDARD TIME at point of origin. Time of receipt is STANDARD TIME at

LDT 1MM 80 GOVT

WASHINGTON DC 1204A DEC 21 1941

MRS GENEVIEVE DUNLAP

3545 LINDA VISTA TERRACE LOSA-

THE NAVY DEPARTMENT DEEPLY REGRETS TO INFORM YOU THAT YOUR SONS WESLEY JOHN HEIDT FIREMAN FIRST CLASS US NAVY AND EDWARD JOSEPH HEIDT FIREMAN FIRST CLASS US NAVY ARE MISSING FOLLOWING ACTION IN THE PERFORMANCE OF THEIR DUTY AND IN THE SERVICE OF THEIR COUNTRY X THE DEPARTMENT APPRECIATES YOUR GREAT ANXIETY AND WILL FURNISH YOU FURTHER INFORMATION PROMPTLY WHEN RECEIVED X TO POSSIBLE AID TO OUR ENEMIES PLEASE DO NOT DI

SHIP OR STATION

The USS *Arizona* Memorial was built over the middle of the sunken battleship, which is visible through the water. About 1.5 million people visit the site every year.

The next morning, Garcia returned to the harbor. He joined rescue teams trying to free sailors trapped inside the battleships and worked with them for several weeks.

The attacks on Pearl Harbor were devastating. More than 2,400 Americans died and another 1,178 were wounded. But because of hundreds of dedicated rescuers like Garcia, DeCastro, and Erickson, many lives were saved.

The following day, the United States entered World War II.

Genevieve Dunlap was the mother of two sailors aboard the *Arizona*, Wesley and Edward Heidt. She received this telegram informing her that her sons were missing in action. Later she learned that they had died.

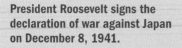
President Roosevelt signs the declaration of war against Japan on December 8, 1941.

THE U.S. ENTERS THE WAR

On December 8, 1941, President Franklin D. Roosevelt signed a declaration of war against Japan. In a speech to Congress, he declared December 7 "a date which will live in infamy." Then he reached out to the Allies to join the fight against the Axis powers.

After two long years of watching and waiting, Americans quickly mobilized for war. Millions of young men signed up for military service. Women took their

Women at work in an aircraft factory in Tennessee in 1942

places in factories that by the end of the war would churn out 2,700 transport ships, 299,293 planes, 634,569 jeeps, and 40 billion bullets.

In February 1942, war fervor mingled with fear and racial hatred, leading President Roosevelt to order the internment of all Japanese Americans living on the West Coast. National Guard troops forced more than 110,000 Japanese Americans into prison camps. Many of these innocent citizens would spend the rest of the war behind barbed wire.

In the weeks after the attack on Pearl Harbor, Japanese forces swept through Southeast Asia and the Pacific. European colonies quickly fell to the Japanese. And by May, Japan had captured the Philippines.

In June, Japanese Admiral Isoroku Yamamoto sent his fleet to seize Midway, a tiny island in the middle of the Pacific. An invasion force based there would put Japan within striking distance of Hawaii.

But three American aircraft carriers, accompanied by seven cruisers, met the fleet and launched a massive battle to halt the Japanese advance. "A beautiful silver waterfall" of dive bombers, in the words of one American pilot, descended on the Japanese fleet. When the smoke cleared, four of Yamamoto's six aircraft carriers—and his plans for a quick end to the war—had been destroyed.

The Mochida family on their way to an internment camp. Japanese Americans were imprisoned because the U.S. government feared they would side with Japan. However, none were ever found guilty of sabotage.

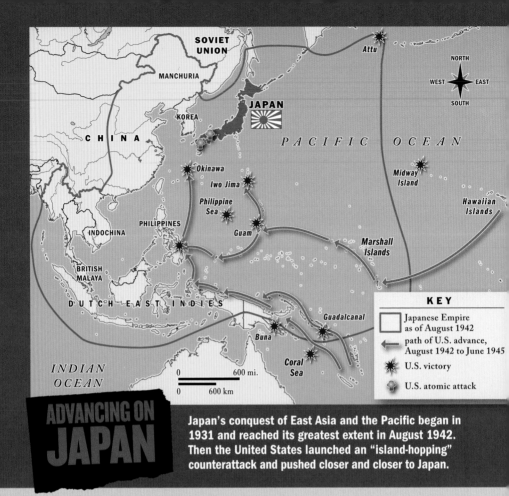

SOVIET
UNION

MANCHURIA

Attu

NORTH

WEST ✦ EAST

SOUTH

KOREA

CHINA

JAPAN

PACIFIC OCEAN

Okinawa

Iwo Jima

Midway
Island

Philippine
Sea

Hawaiian
Islands

PHILIPPINES

INDOCHINA

Guam

Marshall
Islands

BRITISH
MALAYA

DUTCH EAST INDIES

Guadalcanal

KEY

Buna

INDIAN
OCEAN

0   600 mi.

0   600 km

Coral
Sea

◻ Japanese Empire
as of August 1942

← path of U.S. advance,
August 1942 to June 1945

✸ U.S. victory

⬢ U.S. atomic attack

ADVANCING ON JAPAN

Japan's conquest of East Asia and the Pacific began in
1931 and reached its greatest extent in August 1942.
Then the United States launched an "island-hopping"
counterattack and pushed closer and closer to Japan.

As U.S. forces battled in the Pacific, war was still raging on the
other side of the world. Hitler's troops now ranged through Western
Europe, into the Soviet Union, and across the deserts of North
Africa.

But in late 1942, the momentum began to shift. In November,
an Allied invasion force landed in North Africa. By May 1943, the
Allies had defeated the Axis armies there.

On June 6, 1944, the Allies
sent 175,000 troops into
heavy fire on the beaches of
Normandy, France.

Allied troops land in Normandy
on D-Day—June 6, 1944.

Over the next months, millions of British, Canadian, and American troops swept through France and closed in on Germany from the west. The Soviet Red Army pressed in from the east. After five years of war, the Allies finally had Hitler surrounded.

In the Pacific, U.S. forces slowly regained lost territory. With Australia as a base, U.S. Marines moved west toward the Philippines and north toward Japan. They seized island after island, clawing their way onto beaches in brutal fighting. By the spring of 1945, U.S. troops were in striking distance of Japan.

Finally, in May 1945, Germany surrendered to the Allies. But despite massive bombing raids on its cities, Japan refused to surrender.

Then, on August 6, 1945, a B-29 bomber named the *Enola Gay* dropped a single atomic bomb on the Japanese city of Hiroshima. The explosion brought instant death to 70,000 people. Burns and radiation would double that death toll by the end of the year.

On August 9, a second mushroom cloud rose over Nagasaki.

Six days later, its people hungry and broken, Japan surrendered, bringing to a close the most devastating war in history.

The ruins of Hiroshima, Japan, after it was destroyed by an atomic bomb

TIMELINE

1931: Japan invades the Chinese province of Manchuria.

1933: Adolf Hitler becomes chancellor of Germany. He turns Germany into a police state with himself as its all-powerful leader.

1937: Japan conquers Nanking, the capital of China, and massacres 200,000 Chinese civilians.

1938: The U.S. begins a massive build-up of its navy.

1939: World War II begins when Germany invades Poland. France and Britain react by declaring war on Germany.

1940: Germany conquers France and other Western European nations.

1940: Japan allies itself with the Axis powers (Germany and Italy) and occupies Indochina.

1941: Germany invades the Soviet Union.

1941: Japan attacks the U.S. fleet at Pearl Harbor, Hawaii. The U.S. declares war on Japan. It also joins Britain and the other Allies in the war against Germany.

1942: The U.S. government orders the imprisonment of more than 110,000 Japanese Americans.

1942: The U.S. defeats Japan at the Battle of Midway, turning the war's momentum against Japan.

1943: After defeating Axis armies in North Africa, the Allies invade Italy.

1944: The Allies land in Normandy, France, and begin to advance on Germany.

1945: U.S. planes firebomb Tokyo and other Japanese cities, causing great damage and killing hundreds of thousands of civilians.

1945: Allied troops sweep into Germany from the east and west. On April 30, Adolf Hitler commits suicide. Eight days later, Germany surrenders, ending the war in Europe.

1945: On August 6 and 9, the U.S. drops atomic bombs on Hiroshima and Nagasaki, killing more than 220,000 Japanese people. On August 15, Japan surrenders, ending World War II.

RESOURCES

BOOKS

Adams, Simon. *World War II (DK Eyewitness Books)*. New York: DK Publishing, 2007.

Allen, Thomas B. *Remember Pearl Harbor: Japanese and American Survivors Tell Their Stories.* Washington, DC: National Geographic Children's Books, 2001.

Ambrose, Stephen E. *The Good Fight: How World War II Was Won*. New York: Atheneum, 2001.

Fitzgerald, Stephanie. *Pearl Harbor: Day of Infamy*. Minneapolis: Compass Point Books, 2006.

Gorman, Jacqueline Laks. *Pearl Harbor: A Primary Source History (In Their Own Words)*. Pleasantville, NY: Gareth Stevens Publishing, 2009.

Hoyt, Edwin P. *Pearl Harbor Attack*. New York: Sterling Point Books, 2008.

McGowen, Tom. *The Attack on Pearl Harbor (Cornerstones of Freedom, Second Series)*. New York: Children's Press, 2007.

Nicholson, Dorinda Makanaonalani. *Pearl Harbor Child: A Child's View of Pearl Harbor from Attack to Peace*. Kansas City, MO: Woodson House Publishing, 2001.

Rice Jr., Earle. *The Attack on Pearl Harbor*. San Diego: Lucent Books, 1997.

Tanaka, Shelley. *Attack on Pearl Harbor: The True Story of the Day America Entered World War II*. New York: Scholastic, 2002.

WEBSITES

The National World War II Museum
http://www.nationalww2 museum.org
The National World War II Museum in New Orleans tells the story of American involvement in World War II through personal accounts, artifacts, documents, photographs, and film footage.

The Pearl Harbor Attack, 7 December 1941
http://www.history.navy.mil/faqs/faq66-1.htm
This Naval Historical Center site is full of facts and statistics about the attack on Pearl Harbor.

Remembering Pearl Harbor, December 7, 1941
http://plasma.national geographic.com/pearlharbor
This *National Geographic* site includes photos, timelines, a multimedia map of the attack, stories by survivors, and an account of an underwater expedition at the battle site in 2000.

USS *Arizona* Memorial
http://www.nps.gov/archive/usar/home.htm
Find out about the National Park Service memorial built above the sunken USS *Arizona*.

World War II Valor in the Pacific National Monument
http://www.nps.gov/valr/index.htm
More about the USS *Arizona* Memorial and the history of Pearl Harbor.

DICTIONARY

A

aircraft carrier (AIR-kraft KA-ree-ur) *noun* a warship with a large, flat deck that aircraft use to take off and land

alliance (uh-LYE-uhnss) *noun* an agreement to join forces and work together

Allies (AL-eyes) *noun* the alliance of nations that fought against the Axis powers during World War II; the three major Allied powers were the United States, Great Britain, and the Soviet Union

altitude (AL-ti-tood) *noun* the height of something above the ground or water

ammunition hold (am-yuh-NISH-uhn HOLD) *noun* the place on a ship where ammunition is stored

anti-aircraft gun (AN-tee-AIR-kraft gun) *noun* a large gun designed to shoot down enemy aircraft

Axis (AK-siss) *noun* the alliance of nations opposed to the Allies during World War II; the three major Axis powers were Germany, Italy, and Japan

C

capsize (KAP-size) *verb* to turn over in the water

casualty (KAZH-oo-uhl-tee) *noun* someone who is killed, injured, imprisoned, or missing in action during a war

D

democracy (di-MOK-ruh-see) *noun* a system of government in which the people choose their leaders in free elections

dictator (DIK-tay-tur) *noun* a leader who has total authority over a country, often ruling through intimidation or force

dogfight (DAWG-fite) *noun* an aerial battle between fighter planes

F

fuselage (FYOO-suh-lahzh) *noun* the main body of an aircraft

H

hangar (HANG-ur) *noun* a large building where aircraft are kept

hull (HUHL) *noun* the frame or body of a boat or ship

I

infamy (IN-fuh-mee) *noun* an evil reputation brought about by an extremely criminal, shocking, or brutal act

internment (in-TURN-mint) *noun* the confinement of people without trial, for political or military reasons

isolationist (eye-soh-LAY-shun-ist) *noun* a person who wants his or her country to avoid involvement in the political and military affairs of other countries

M

mess attendant (MESS uh-TEN-dent) *noun* during World War II, a sailor who worked as a servant to officers on a ship; duties often included preparing meals, doing laundry, and cleaning living quarters

midget submarine (MIJ-it SUHB-muh-reen) *noun* a small submarine operated by a crew of only one or two people

minelayer (MINE-lay-uhr) *noun* a ship that places explosive devices in the water to destroy ships or submarines

morphine (MORE-feen) *noun* a very strong painkiller

S

strafe (STRAYF) *verb* to attack with machine-gun fire from low-flying aircraft

T

torpedo (tor-PEE-doh) *noun* an underwater missile that explodes when it hits a target

U

U-boat (YOO BOTE) *noun* a German submarine used during World War I and World War II

V

vulnerable (VUHL-nur-uh-buhl) *adjective* susceptible to physical or emotional harm

INDEX

ABOUT THIS BOOK

As I researched the Japanese attack on Pearl Harbor, the words of eyewitnesses brought the event to life for me. Reading their stories, I felt as though I was engulfed by the fire and smoke. I could feel the ground shake from the explosions. I could smell the burning fuel and the seared flesh. And I could feel people's panic as they tried desperately to hide from the diving fighter planes.

The eyewitness accounts also conveyed the courage of the men and women who fought back, risking their lives not only for their friends and comrades—but for total strangers as well.

The story of Dorie Miller, who could only serve in the U.S. Navy as a kitchen helper because he was black, illustrates how dramatically American life has changed since December 7, 1941. Twenty-one years after Miller fought back so bravely at Pearl Harbor, Barack Obama was born a few miles away in Honolulu. He would go on to become the first African American president of the United States.

The following books and websites were helpful while writing this book:

Allen, Thomas B. *Remember Pearl Harbor: American and Japanese Survivors Tell Their Stories.* Washington, D.C.: National Geographic Society, 2001.

Friedrich, Otto. *Day of Infamy: 50th Anniversary Special.* New York: TIME, 1991.

Gailey, Harry A. *The War in the Pacific.* New York: Random House, 1997.

Keegan, John. *The Second World War.* New York: Penguin Books, 1990.

Prange, Gordon W. *Dec. 7, 1941: The Day the Japanese Attacked Pearl Harbor.* New York: Warner Books, 1988.

Rice Jr., Earle. *The Attack on Pearl Harbor.* San Diego: Lucent Books, 1997.

Shapiro, William E. *Turning Points of World War II: Pearl Harbor.* New York: Franklin Watts, 1984.

Tanaka, Shelley. *Attack on Pearl Harbor: The True Story of the Day America Entered World War II.* New York: Scholastic, 2002.

Terkel, Studs. *The Good War: An Oral History of World War II.* New York: Random House, 1984.

U.S. Department of the Navy. *Oral Histories of the Pearl Harbor Attack.* Washington, D.C.: Naval Historical Center Online Library, 2009.

www.pearlharborsurvivorsonline.org/Index%20Page%20.htm
www.pearlharborstories.org
www.arizonamemorial.org
plasma.nationalgeographic.com/pearlharbor

—Steve Dougherty